Heiner Müller
The Hamletma...

"I'm good Hamlet gi'me a cause for grief."

At first glance, readers of *The Hamletmachine* (1979) could be forgiven for wondering whether it is actually a play at all: it opens with a montage of texts that are not ascribed to a character, there is no vestige of a plot and the whole piece lasts a total of ten pages.

Yet, **Heiner Müller's** play regularly features in the theatres' repertoires and is frequently staged by university theatre departments. David Barnett examines why such a seemingly obscure piece has proved so popular, introducing readers to Müller as an experimental, politically committed writer who confronts the shortcomings of his age in a compact and radically open play.

In four short, accessible chapters, this lively book unpicks the complexities of *The Hamletmachine's* writing, considers the problems Müller poses for its performance and discusses two exemplary productions in order to show how the play can engage very different audiences.

David Barnett is a Professor of Theatre at the University of York.

The Fourth Wall

The Fourth Wall series is a growing collection of short books on famous plays. Its compact format perfectly suits the kind of fresh, engaging criticism that brings a play to life.

Each book in this series selects one play or musical as its subject and approaches it from an original angle, seeking to shed light on an old favourite or break new ground on a modern classic. These lively, digestible books are a must for anyone looking for new ideas on the major works of modern theatre.

Also available in this series:

Coming soon:

Heiner Müller's
The Hamletmachine

David Barnett

Routledge
Taylor & Francis Group

LONDON AND NEW YORK

First published 2016
by Routledge
2 Park Square, Milton Park, Abingdon, Oxon OX14 4RN

and by Routledge
711 Third Avenue, New York, NY 10017

Routledge is an imprint of the Taylor & Francis Group, an informa business

© 2016 David Barnett

The right of David Barnett to be identified as author of this
work has been asserted by him in accordance with sections 77
and 78 of the Copyright, Designs and Patents Act 1988.

British Library Cataloguing-in-Publication Data
A catalogue record for this book is available from
the British Library

Library of Congress Cataloguing-in-Publication Data
A catalog record for this title has been requested

ISBN: 9781138192775 (pbk)
ISBN: 9781315639673 (ebk)

Typeset in Bembo
by Out of House Publishing

Contents

Introduction

The playwright

Heiner Müller was born in Eppendorf, a village in the German province of Saxony, in 1929, and died in the nation's capital, Berlin, in 1995, aged 66. In the early 1990s, he noted with typical irony: 'it's a privilege for a writer to see the demise of three states in one lifetime. The Weimar Republic, the Fascist State and the German Democratic Republic [GDR]. I doubt I'll experience the fall of the Federal Republic any more.'[1] As is evident, the playwright lived through a great deal of upheaval, but what is perhaps more important is that he drew on the seismic shifts in German and European history as material for his work.

While Müller, at the age of 4, may not have been that conscious of the fall of the Weimar Republic, he certainly felt the full force of Nazi barbarism at a young age. His father, a Social Democrat, was arrested by the Nazis and interned in a concentration camp for political prisoners before being released after a number of months. Müller was 16 at the close of the Second World War and chose to remain in the GDR,

Germany's socialist state, when his parents fled west to the Federal Republic of Germany in 1951. It was the GDR that introduced him to the contradictions of socialism, a system he at once supported and scrutinized. He found that his plays were often censured, cancelled or banned, yet he would never give up his commitment to progressive politics and social justice.

By the time the Berlin Wall was opened in November 1989, Müller was already a writer with an international reputation and was free to travel the world, a privilege shared by only handful of fellow citizens of the GDR. Germany was reunified in October 1990, and this effectively marked the start of a lean period for a productive playwright. The tensions between East and West, between socialism and capitalism, were dissipating, and in this time of rapid transition, he found himself without the historical and political material that had previously driven his work. Instead, he became a member of a five-man management team at the Berliner Ensemble (the City of Berlin appointed no women), the theatre company co-founded by his most important influence, Bertolt Brecht. By 1995, in-fighting had led Müller to assume sole control. His reign did not last long, however: weakened by treatment for cancer of the gullet, he died on 30 December.

Müller started writing at an early age and helped found a collective of young authors in 1948. His breakthrough as a playwright came in 1957 when he, together with his wife, Inge, wrote a play about a record-breaking worker called *The Wage Sinker*. While one might suppose that it was a simple celebration of heroic labour, the play is anything but: Balke, the productive innovator, was just as dedicated a worker under the Nazis as he was under socialism, and his efforts, as the play's title suggests, are detrimental to his colleagues. This play already displays Müller's keenness to identify and expose contradictions that need to be confronted if change is to take place.

Müller continued to set his plays in the GDR, yet when one was cancelled after its first performance in 1961, the year the Berlin Wall was erected, and another was effectively banned before it could reach the stage in 1965, he turned his attention to ancient Greek myths as a way of dealing with the problems of the present. His version of *Philoctetes* (1965),[2] for example, returns to Sophocles's play and uses the three main figures to represent different political positions. Odysseus brings Neoptolemus to the island of Lemnos, on which Philoctetes has been abandoned, together with his magic bow and arrows. The pair seek to convince Philoctetes through deception to part with the weapon they think might turn the Trojan War in their favour. In Müller's version, Odysseus is the political pragmatist, prepared to use any means necessary to secure his ends; Neoptolemus his zealous accomplice; and Philoctetes the embittered and aggrieved victim of other people's decisions.

The radical re-employment of historical and cultural material went on to inform other plays. The role of Shakespeare became increasingly visible, too, from the Hamlet-like character Hasselbein in a play set in the GDR, *The Building Site* (1965), to an adaptation of *Macbeth* (1972) and the hybrid work *Anatomy Titus Fall of Rome: A Shakespeare Commentary* (1985). Elsewhere, *Germania Death in Berlin* (1977) mostly pairs up scenes from the GDR with parallels from mythology, literature and history in a montage that both draws parallels and points to discrepancies within thematically related material.

Müller was something of a magpie: he plundered sources and ideas wherever he found them and used them to create tensions and contradictions in his plays. His work became increasingly associative, floating above potential meanings, and the writing itself offered little to illuminate his own views on the themes he chose to explore.

The play

Before considering the play to which this book is dedicated, it is worth lingering on its title. The two major translations in English call it *Hamletmachine* and *The Hamletmachine*.[3] The German original contains the definite article – *Die Hamletmaschine* – and although this might appear to be a minor detail, its retention in English is not insignificant. *Hamletmachine* lends itself to a sense of generality; *The Hamletmachine* is more specific and anchors the phenomena encountered in the text to the figures and the situations on stage. That is, *Hamletmachine* could be construed as having universal applicability; *The Hamletmachine* suggests that it is concerned with the particular configurations of speech and action set out in the play.

This may seem like nit-picking, yet it goes to the heart of some central political and philosophical issues that Müller worked through in his career. Broadly speaking, Müller was a Marxist. This is a contention to which I will return in Chapter 3, but, for the time being, I will merely note that Marxists argue that human beings are always influenced by their place in society and history. So, the way that, say, men think about women will be different if the men in question live in Norway or Namibia, in the twenty-first century or in the twentieth. This relationship between individual, society and history affects the way that people make judgements and act. The preservation of the definite article in the play's title suggests that we pay attention to the specificities of the text and its contexts.

The Hamletmachine was written and published in 1977. The ten-page play was not, however, published as a book or even as part of an anthology; instead it appeared in a programme for another play, *Oedipus the King*. And this production took place in Munich, in West Germany, not in the GDR. This aspect is not that surprising: the GDR authorities would have found the text to be far too experimental and divergent from their own pronouncements on the form and function of literature to have been allowed to appear in the East at that time. Indeed, it was only published there in 1988, a time at which artistic liberalization had finally arrived in the GDR.

Müller's notes, held in his archive in Berlin, reveal that the original working title was *Hamlet in Budapest*.[4] Again, there is a specificity to this conception: it sets up a concrete relationship between a Hamlet figure and a particularly fraught period in the history of workers' politics. The Hungarian Uprising of 1956 marked a time in which Soviet tanks enforced a particular definition of communism in a country seeking to develop its own interpretation. What remain in the finished play are a direct reference to Hungary in part of the fourth scene's title, 'Pest in Buda', and allusions in the description of an uprising in the same scene. Like much of the rest of the play, suggestive material has more power to create associations among the different thematic elements that run through the scenes.

The decision to call the play *The Hamletmachine* and not *Hamlet in Budapest* provokes questions and associations, too. The former strike at the very heart of human endeavour: what is the balance between the human and the mechanical? To what extent do we have control over our actions? These issues connect the title with Andy Warhol, a pioneer of pop art, who asked in an interview with *Time* magazine in 1963: 'I'd like to be a machine, wouldn't you?'.[5] His point is that life would be far easier if everything were automated, a position not dissimilar to that of the Hamlet figure in the play. Finally, Müller also references a section of Marcel Duchamp's *The Large Glass*, the 'Bachelor Machine'. This is another example of a work that questions human autonomy, here more specifically in the sphere of human desire and social conformity.

As Müller noted in an interview in 1981: 'the first preoccupation I have when I write drama is to destroy things. For thirty years Hamlet was a real obsession for me, so I tried to destroy him by writing a short text, [*The*] *Hamletmachine*.'[6] This impulse informs the play in many ways and these will be addressed in the following chapters. Chapter 1 offers an overview of the complex work, pointing out the dramaturgical features that make it so distinctive. Chapter 2 digs a little deeper into the dense matrix of sources that informs the scenes, and outlines their functions. Chapter 3 considers questions of genre, whether *The Hamletmachine* can still be understood as a drama, and how a change of status might affect the play's reception. Chapter 4 describes and reflects on two different approaches to staging the play in a bid to compass some of the possibilities open to directors and actors. The Conclusion then speculates on the future of the play.

Notes

1   Heiner Müller, *Krieg ohne Schlacht: Eine Autobiographie*, in Müller, *Werke*, Vol. IX, ed. Frank Hörnigk (Frankfurt am Main: Suhrkamp, 2005), pp. 7–291 (p. 283). All translations from the German are mine, unless otherwise acknowledged.

2 This and subsequent dates denote first year of publication.

3 Heiner Müller, *'Hamletmachine' and Other Texts for the Stage*, trans. and ed. Carl Weber (Baltimore: Performing Arts Journal Publications, 1984), and Heiner Müller, *Theatremachine*, trans. and ed. Marc von Henning (London: Faber and Faber, 1995), respectively. I will be using Henning's translation in this book.

4 Heiner Müller Archive, item 3887.

5 Andy Warhol, quoted in Eric Shanes, *Andy Warhol* (London: Sirrocco, n.d.), p. 30. Müller directly references the connection in Heiner Müller Archive, item 3887.

6 Sylvère Lotringer and Heiner Müller, 'Walls', in Müller, *Germania*, trans. and annot. Bernard and Caroline Schütze, ed. Lotringer (New York: Semiotext(e), 1990), pp. 13–61 (pp. 55–6).

Surveying the scenes

The Hamletmachine is a striking text for a number of fairly obvious reasons. It is remarkably short: in the original and in translation, it barely reaches ten pages. It is, however, a complete play, and theatre-makers have to confront the question of how something so slender will engender a full production. Then, one has the problem of the scenes themselves: Müller does not make them easy to understand and their presentation is unusual, to say the least. This chapter focuses on their construction and deals with the peculiarities of each scene in turn before assessing the ways they work when taken together.

I 'Family Album'

Unlike all the other scenes, this one attributes no character name to the different types of text that follow. From the very outset, actors have no inkling as to who is speaking. This already difficult position is further problematized by the opening sentence, 'I was Hamlet.'[1] The speaker, whose identity is already a mystery, may no longer be Hamlet. A formulation like 'I have been Hamlet' would have marked a boundary: I have been, but am no longer. 'I was Hamlet' is not that definitive; the possibility of continuation is still present in the employment of the simple past tense in both the German original and the English translation.

It is worth dwelling on the first sentence because it is disorientating and open. The three opening words already propose a dynamic model of human identity, one capable of change. In past productions, the scene has been spoken by a single Hamlet figure; a single Ophelia; and several voices, split and in chorus. Each choice offers a different interpretation: that Hamlet cannot cast off his identity, that Ophelia can, or that identity is actually a multifaceted thing that has its various emphases and modes. Each permutation reflects a different model of what a self may be, yet we should not forget that Müller refuses to offer an answer of his own; the work is to be done by the theatre.

The scene hardly clarifies matters after its first sentence. A quick read reveals that it is composed of formally different blocks of text. The opening paragraph reflects on a funeral. The mention of Hamlet in the first line already suggests that it is the funeral of Hamlet's father, Old Hamlet, who was murdered by his brother, Claudius, in Shakespeare's play. The action described in the past tense does not occur in *Hamlet* and, to make things even more confusing, there are lines in the present tense, presented in block capitals. This temporal tension may suggest memories of the funeral breaking their way into the speaker's attempt to tell a story, a past that will not go away. Yet that interpretation only applies if a production is employing a single speaker. The use of more voices does not pin such a reading to an individual.

The next section appears exclusively in block capitals and moves away from the variation on the *Hamlet* story that precedes it. In the German original, six of the eight lines are given in English. It is clear that block capitals signify something, but precisely what they might mean is never revealed by the text itself. The eight lines seem disconnected from each other, some reflecting on the speaking self, some on the state of the world. Again, it is disjunction and instability that pervade the passage.

The following section, presented exclusively in conventional type, is mostly delivered in the present tense: it is a dialogue between the speaker(s) and Old Hamlet's ghost, except that the ghost does not speak a single word.

A pattern then seems to emerge, in that another section of block capitals follows. Yet, thematically, it is quite different from the first one. This one takes the form of a poem and employs a lyric 'I'. The earlier fragmentary material is replaced by something with a little more coherence. The final section then returns to the allusions to the *Hamlet* story and is also interspersed with lines in block capitals.

So, what can be said about this peculiar opening scene? Its textual strategy aims to make one of the basic relationships in theatre problematic in that it is impossible to decide who is speaking the texts. From this unknowable position, the text itself assumes a special status. By refusing to attribute a speaker to the words, Müller no longer proposes a link between text and character. The text is thus allowed to 'float' above possible meanings without being attached to a particular person or identity. This raises questions about agency, of who does what. It is usually assumed that people who speak texts are in some way the texts' masters: they determine what is said. However, on closer reflection, this only tells half the story. Any speaker, in even the most conventional of plays, is subject to a set of rules that determine what can and cannot be said. These are the rules of grammar, primarily, but also those of usage, of how words are deployed to create meaning. While grammar and usage both evolve over time, they nonetheless constrain any speaker's ability to make sense. Anyone who has learned a foreign language will know that there are some things that can be expressed simply in one language, but not in another. In addition, speakers rarely create their own words. With the exception of neologisms, we use words because we have heard or read them elsewhere. As a result, we always reuse words and are limited by the meanings attached to them by other people in other places. It may then be the case that words 'speak' us, rather than us speaking words. This has important implications for agency: we are more limited in what we can express and, by extension, do. This aspect signals a connection with the play's title: in what proportion is a person both a self-determining human being and a pre-programmed machine?

Müller's opening scene highlights this problem by refusing to attribute a speaker to the spoken and by undermining the thematic and formal coherence of the scene. However, while the playwright signals that all language is 'second-hand' by definition, his remarkable use of words shows what can be done with language nonetheless. His acknowledgement of its restrictions and its reach points to a contradiction that runs through human identity: we are both imitative and original at the same time. This is an important corrective to the apparent autonomy granted to individuals in drama. Müller tempers this idea by revealing everyone's debt to the past, a motif to which I will return in Chapter 2.

It is tempting to read the five sections of the scene as the five acts of *Hamlet*, but there is no correlation between Shakespeare's action and the texts of 'Family Album'. At most, one might understand the format as a nod to Shakespeare's five-act structure and remember Müller's interest in textual destruction: this is what is left of classical dramaturgy in 1977. That the five acts still survive echoes the precarious opening, 'I was Hamlet': they are present, but in such a different form that one has to ask what function they might still serve. I will return to this question at the end of this chapter.

2 'Europe of the Woman'

This scene is markedly shorter than 'Family Album'. Its title is, at least partially, specific: it is not 'The Life of the Woman', but focuses on a geo-political category: Europe. This is not, then, about women's struggles in general, but about the struggle within a particular context. Müller is not trying to address the developing world or even North America – he is constructing a network of connections that draw on Europe's past in order to influence Europe's future. This does not mean, of course, that *The Hamletmachine* cannot be performed elsewhere: its production history refutes that position. But just as an American classic like *A Streetcar Named Desire* can play worldwide, directors and producers should be sensitive to this play's origins and concerns here, too.

The scene opens with some odd stage directions: '*Enormous room. Ophelia. Her heart is a clock*' (89). The opening spatial designation is also a reference to E. E. Cummings's *The Enormous Room*, a semi-autobiographical novel dealing with his internment in France during the First World War. The direction is thus both literal and metaphorical. The following mention of a character by name may give the impression that the play is starting to return to more conventional dramaturgical practice, yet the scene's character attribution, 'OPHELIA

[CHORUS/HAMLET]' (89), already dispels the impression that Müller has chosen to stabilize his notion of character. The invitation to turn the monologue that follows into a choric text undermines the dominance of the Ophelia figure, despite the opening line 'I am Ophelia' (89). The switch from past ('I was Hamlet') to present is clearly significant, yet the inclusion of a 'HAMLET' in the attribution suggests that things may be a little more complicated. The final part of the stage direction is an example of a feature that will recur in excess in the following scene: it is an image that defies the design team to stage it because it is metaphorical and not literal. Of course, designers could indeed hang a clock around Ophelia's neck or attach an emblem above her heart, yet such literalism is not in keeping with the associative nature of the rest of the text. If the direction is not to be represented visually, one has to wonder what one does with it. I shall turn to this question in the discussion of Scene 3, below.

The speech itself is not as fragmented as 'Family Album'. Indeed, it moves clearly from an identification of Ophelia with other female suicides, via the decision to stop 'killing myself' (89), to a series of described actions involving the destruction of the domestic sphere, a radicalization of the self and a move from the private to the public. This coherence, as discussed in the following chapter, is not unproblematic.

'Ophelia', the apparently singular speaker, assumes a collective identity in the opening lines. This is no longer an individual, but a type. As such, the repeated use of an 'I' that follows has the power of more than one voice. This was already acknowledged in the attribution at the start of the scene, but it is not a chorus of equals that delivers the lines. For one, Hamlet is male, and so the sincerity of his delivery is called into question. Is this an attempt to sympathize with the woman who killed herself in response to his actions in Shakespeare's *Hamlet*? Is he trying to assuage his guilt? Is this the tokenistic behaviour of a liberal? The answer, which the text does not give, is perhaps not important; rather, it is the fact that Hamlet is actually speaking the Ophelia lines that is significant.

3 'Scherzo'

'Scherzo' is a term taken from classical music. It is an Italian word that means 'a joke' and often denotes a comic movement in a larger work. By setting the scene thus, Müller gestures to a contrast between the subject matter and its performance.

The scene is almost entirely composed of stage directions that evoke a grotesque or nightmarish scene. In part they refer back to the description of the female suicides in 'Europe of the Woman'. While some of the directions are potentially performable, as when Hamlet views the dead women with the distance of a visitor at a museum, others are not. '*On a swing the Madonna with breast cancer.* [. . .] *The breast cancer shines like a sun*' (90) defies literal representation and, like the opening to the previous scene, may suggest that Müller is trying to do something other with his stage directions than simply have them performed, as is usually the case when scripts offer descriptions of scenes, costumes, entrances and exits. That is, the stage directions may have a similar status to the spoken text in a play like this. Neither type of text maps easily onto the conventional modes of delivery and performance. Müller is perhaps proposing a different kind of theatre through his use of text in the play as a whole. If the stage directions are not to be acted out, then maybe they are to be presented in a different form. Productions have spoken and projected such texts, and in doing this, they transfer the responsibility for interpreting the images from the production to the audience. Such approaches thus retain the openness of the directions and invite the spectators to reconcile the lines with the rest of the decisions the production team and the actors have taken.

The 'Scherzo' is also the only scene that includes figures other than Hamlet and Ophelia, and contains the only dialogue in the entire play. It is worth noting, however, that the 'dialogue' can hardly be considered a conversation. While Ophelia's call may elicit a response from Hamlet, there is little to establish much of a relationship. In the nightmarish context of the scene, the exchange of lines may indicate a parody of communication rather than a meaningful exchange of positions.

This scene has a special status in *The Hamletmachine* in that it appears at the play's centre. Formally, it is different from the other four in that it features little text to be spoken, is dominated by stage directions and is framed by a comic term. In archival notes to the play, Müller called it a 'dream within a dream'.[2]

4 'Pest in Buda/Battle of Greenland'

The reference to Budapest in the title of this scene directly relates it to the Hungarian Uprising of 1956, as does the monologue that opens with 'The set is a monument' (91). The word 'pest' echoes an older use of the word in English, that of pestilence, which is its usual meaning in the German original. 'Battle of Greenland' is more enigmatic as, historically, there has never been such a military conflict. Instead, the location suggests a western limit to the themes of the scene, again placing the subject matter in a European context.

Additionally, a battle for a barren land suggests pointlessness. The scene is set in the same space as the second scene; the stage directions indicate that the room has been destroyed. An empty suit of armour is also seen and there is an axe in its helmet, a direct reference back to Old Hamlet in 'Family Album'. Thus, when the Hamletperformer is told to climb into the armour at the end of the scene, he is symbolically becoming his father rather than breaking the old cycle of murder and revenge. However, as in earlier scenes, scepticism towards a literal performance of the stage directions may be in order: is it better to represent the devastated room or the clamber into the armour, or to allow the audience to engage its imagination?

The speaker of the lines appears to be relatively clear: he starts as 'HAMLET', then takes off his '*mask[3] and costume*', and becomes the 'HAMLETPERFORMER' (90). That is, the attribution of character to text takes the form of a denial, a negation of a role. The problem is whether the audience can accept the sincerity of the gesture. Hamlet wants to cast off his role, but, as the final stage direction indicates, he re-assumes it. Much of the text plays with Hamlet's vacillation and difficulty in committing to the uprising he describes. So, once again, Müller problematizes the question of who is actually speaking, even though in this section it seems to be evident.

The spoken text opens with a now familiar format: a mixture of conventionally written lines and ones in block capitals. They provoke the denial of the role, couched in the language of the theatre. Hamlet, an actor in Shakespeare when he feigns madness, seeks authenticity, but finds that he cannot escape role-playing. The monologue that then describes the uprising is framed by stagehands who set up a scene of hollow domesticity: a fridge and three televisions. The description is interspersed with narration, comment and more poetic reflections on the situation that culminate in the contradictory juxtaposition of the Hamletperformer seeing himself 'on both sides of the front' (91) yet returning home 'at one with my undivided self' (92). What follows is a self-loathing reflection on modern life in a consumer society, rendered as a poem, and fragmentary lines that lead to the Hamletperformer's return to his role as Hamlet.

Stage directions instruct three naked women to enter the stage as Marx, Lenin and Mao, before Hamlet, as he is after reapplying his make-up and re-donning his costume, cleaves their skulls in two with the axe. Again, the directions resist literal performance: is a designer really going to devise a device to present such an action? However, in the midst of the scene, there is one stage direction that has regularly been staged in many of productions of the play: '*A photograph of the writer*', followed by '[the Hamletperformer] *tears up the photograph of the writer*' (93). This pair of instructions can, of course, be treated like all the others, as evocative text, yet the immediacy of the action and its visual impact have clearly appealed to many a director over the years. The meaning of the gesture has elicited various interpretations. Some critics note that this is Müller questioning his right to call himself the author of such a heterogeneous work,[4] something discussed in the next chapter. Others, such as Doris Perl, understand that 'the efforts of the author to eliminate his own privileges emanate from a privileged position themselves'.[5] Both explanations point to the paradoxical place of such writing: Müller signals both the originality of the play and its indebtedness to a wealth of sources. The performance of these directions, unlike many of the others, does not reduce their ability to generate associations and questions.

5 'Maddening Endurance/Inside the Dreaded Armour/Millennia'

One of Müller's sources provides the title for the final scene: it is a fragment from a poem by Friedrich Hölderlin. It connects, quite directly, with the final lines of the previous scene and proposes that Hamlet's reversion to brutality and conservatism, the '*ice age*' (93) that concludes 'Pest in Buda', marks a long period of inertia that shows little sign of ending. The consequences of this condition are enacted upon Ophelia as she is wrapped in bandages by two male surgeons. Again, there is a metaphorical scenic setting: Ophelia is in the depths of the ocean and '*fish/wreckage/corpses and limbs drift by*' (94).

As Scene 4 echoes Scene 1, Scene 5 echoes Scene 2. The spoken text is short and relatively clear. Again it includes an 'I', but again the 'I' is problematized. While the play attributes 'OPHELIA' to the speech, the first line marks a transformation: 'Here speaks Electra' (94). An easy opposition between Hamlet and Ophelia breaks down: we know that Hamlet is a role-player, yet here, Ophelia is confirmed as one, too: she identifies herself with a mythical revenger. Is she then tarred with Hamlet's brush? Is her inauthenticity a problem, or is it her choice of role that allows her to work in a more productive way than Hamlet? By the end of *The Hamletmachine* it is difficult to speak of 'authenticity' at all, other than as an illusory term, an Eden that can no longer be returned to. The figures are aggregations of other people's words and have to negotiate the world in that knowledge.

Ophelia delivers a speech suffused with hatred in the face of her own silencing by two men. Ultimately, she is unable to move and presents an ambivalent image: has she been defeated or is her enforced silence a final gesture of defiance? As ever, the stage refuses to adjudicate, and the decision is passed on to the auditorium.

All together now

What is to be made of this peculiar set of scenes? Conventional dramaturgical concepts of character and plot are taken apart, although they are not fully discarded. It may be sensible to talk of the play's 'figures' as a broader term or of a 'Hamlet or Ophelia complex', an aggregation of thoughts and impulses that cannot be tied to a single person. And while too little happens to talk of a plot as such, there is nonetheless a progression through time: 'Family Album' is an exposition of sorts; the introduction of the Ophelia figure in 'Europe of the Woman' prefigures the space of 'Pest in Buda' and her silencing in the final scene. As Müller once put it, not without a certain irony: 'you can read *The Hamletmachine* as a five-act play, quite classical in its dramaturgy'.[6] So, there is a radical questioning of the fundamentals of drama, but a semblance still remains, even in the choice of the division into five scenes.

Müller's play reflects a sentiment he expressed in 1975, two years before he wrote *The Hamletmachine*: 'I fundamentally believe that it's literature's job to resist the theatre.'[7] This simple formulation hides a number of positions regarding the role of the writer in the theatrical process. Müller suggests, following an observation of Brecht's in 1931, that the theatre is an essentially conservative institution that is primarily concerned with turning complex, potentially revolutionary artistic meditations on human experience into packageable commodities that can be sold to and consumed by audiences.

Müller proposes that writers deliver plays that are difficult for theatres to stage. In doing that, the writer provokes the theatre to leave behind its conventional methods and develop new ones. The new methods then confront paying patrons with performances that defy expectations: they have to determine their own relationships to the material. As a result, the playwright can influence the workings of theatres. It would seem ludicrous to conceive of *The Hamletmachine* as a conventional play,[8] and its strength, as borne out by its varied production history, points to the many ways in which it has been conceived of and presented (see Chapter 4 for two divergent examples).

The innovative dramaturgy is also a political strategy. If theatres mostly seek to blunt provocative works by making them consumable, then the unruly text threatens to engage theatres in a different kind of theatre-making. It would be difficult to imagine how a play like *The Hamletmachine* might be staged. A mere reading of the text hardly evokes images of a potential production in a way that, say, a play by Chekhov or Mamet might. As a result, spectators cannot prepare themselves for a production of *The Hamletmachine* (apart from reading reviews of the show beforehand, of course). It offers an experience of the material that, by definition, will radically differ from a reading of the play. As Müller put it in one note: 'end of literature (begin of game)'.[9] Directors and actors have to engage with the text at a far more fundamental level than with more conventional works. So, while we might be surprised by a particular interpretation of a classic text in its treatment of character, action or theme, productions of *The Hamletmachine* can offer wonder in their embodiment of a text that offers precious few clues as to how it is to be staged.

Notes

1 Heiner Müller, *The Hamletmachine*, in Müller, *Theatremachine*, pp. 85–94 (p. 87). All subsequent references to the English translation appear as page numbers after the quotation.

2 Heiner Müller Archive, item 3887.

3 In German, *Maske* tends to refer to make-up in the theatre, and so Henning's translation is more metaphorical here.

4 See, for example, Axel Schalk, *Geschichtsmaschinen: Über den Umgang mit der Historie in der Dramatik des technischen Zeitalters. Eine vergleichende Untersuchung* (Heidelberg: Carl Winter, 1989), p. 220.

5 Doris Perl, '"A Document in Madness": Zu Heiner Müllers Umdeutung der klassischen Charaktere in der *Hamletmaschine*', *Shakespeare Jahrbuch* 128 (1992), 157–70 (p. 162).

6 Heiner Müller, in Rolf Rüth and Petra Schmitz, 'Ein Grund zum Schreiben ist Schadenfreude', in Müller, *Werke*, Vol. X, ed. Frank Hörnigk (Frankfurt am Main: Suhrkamp, 2008), pp. 224–35 (p. 232).

7 Heiner Müller, in Horst Laube, 'Literatur muß dem Theater Widerstand leisten', in Müller, *Werke*, Vol. X, pp. 52–73 (p. 57).

8 Although a recent work does just that. James Thomas treats the text 'using standard methods and terms' and reaches the most remarkable of conclusions (James Thomas, *Script Analysis: For Actors, Directors, and Designers*, 5th edn (Burlington, MA: Focal Press, 2014), p. 326). Thomas employs conventional Stanislavskian language, such as 'given circumstances' and 'super-objective', to offer reductive and literal readings of a play that plainly resists them.

9 Heiner Müller Archive, item 3899. The original is in English.

2

A history of western civilization in ten pages

The reference to *Hamlet* in the title of *The Hamletmachine* is the most obvious signal that the play is keen to draw on sources outside itself. A more detailed examination reveals that Müller's text is also rich in allusion and often deliberately skewed quotation. What emerges is a complex network of connections and interconnections, analogies and contrasts that expand the ambition of such a short play to offer a shrunken mosaic of western civilization. This chapter looks at the presentation, role and function of the many sources that inform the play.

The shadow of Shakespeare, the shadow of Müller

Hamlet clearly looms large in the play. Characters from Shakespeare reappear as figures in Müller. Hamlet may be linked to the *Hamlet* story explicitly in 'Family Album' and by extension through Old Hamlet's armour in 'Pest in Buda', but even here, the events are not always analogous to those in *Hamlet*: there is no state funeral, no barbed dialogue with the Ghost, none of the open misanthropy or misogyny. In *Hamlet*,

Old Hamlet is murdered by poison: here by an axe. The only feature Ophelia shares with her Shakespearean counterpart is her suicide, from which she miraculously rises in 'Europe of the Woman'. In *The Hamletmachine*, Hamlet and Ophelia are rather models of certain types of behaviours. Hamlet is embittered, angry, self-pitying, clever, stupid, poetic, blunt, active and passive. One could add any number of additional adjectives that pick up on the diffuse lines of the scenes. He represents the contradictions of the intellectual, not unlike Shakespeare's Hamlet: fresh back from university in Wittenberg, he has to confront a series of dilemmas. Should he avenge his dead father? Can he trust the Ghost? Can he establish Claudius as the murderer? In Müller, the Hamlet figure is faced with a different set of questions, here regarding issues of political commitment and negotiating the contradictions of modern life. Ophelia returns from the dead suffused with hatred and destruction.

In addition, there is no shortage of allusion to *Hamlet* and other works by Shakespeare in *The Hamletmachine*. For example, the lines 'WASH THE MURDER FROM YOUR FACE MY PRINCE / AND BEGIN MAKING EYES AT THE NEW DENMARK' (88) are not that distant from Gertrude's 'Good Hamlet, cast thy nighted colour off / And let thine eye look like a friend on Denmark' (I.ii.68–9).[1] As with Müller's treatment of Hamlet and Ophelia, this is a resemblance, but not a direct equivalence. The new version is suggestive, perhaps reminding the reader or spectator of the original and then drawing attention to the difference between the two. In the original, Gertrude's lines address Hamlet's mood with respect to his dead father; Müller's enigmatic block capitals are more pointed: the murder is directly addressed – there is no mystery to be solved – and Hamlet is encouraged to get used to the new order. This is a more politicized version of the line, one that employs the mother's voice to bring about obedience and conformity. Other allusions require a less detailed knowledge of the original. 'SOMETHING IS ROTTEN IN THIS AGE OF HOPE' varies the well-known 'Something is rotten in the state of Denmark' (I.iv.90), and it is not difficult to appreciate how the change affects our reading of the line. I will return to the practice of using block capitals later in the chapter.

There is an associative relationship between Müller's and Shakespeare's texts beyond *Hamlet*, too. Named references to Richard III and Macbeth both appear, for example. Yet while the former is quite clear (RICHARD THE THIRD I THE PRINCEKILLING KING' (87)), the latter is curious: 'I WAS MACBETH THE KING OFFERED ME HIS THIRD MISTRESS I KNEW EVERY BIRTHMARK ON HER THIGH' (92). The 'I was' formulation reminds us of 'I was Hamlet', but the detail, not present in *Macbeth*, adds another contour to Müller's Hamletperformer. This line is then followed by a direct reference to Raskolnikov, the central character in Dostoevsky's *Crime and Punishment*, who murders an elderly female pawnbroker. The reader or the spectator is left to ponder the connection between two fictional murderers.

Müller's use of Shakespeare, like most of his other sources, is deliberately angular. It is not schematic and there is no 'key' to unlock some kind of hidden meaning. As the examples above show, the text resolutely puts the emphasis on the audience to make meaning because it divulges neither Müller's motivations nor his intentions. Shakespeare provides a rich stockpile of reference points that Müller plunders liberally. He is not interested in offering an interpretation of

Hamlet, preferring to take it apart, scatter its pieces throughout his short play, and see how his rearrangement might resonate with its audience.

Müller never shied away from quoting his own work, either. The description of female suicides in 'Europe of the Woman' is a direct lift from his play *Life of Gundling Frederick of Prussia Lessing's Sleep Dream* (1977). There is also an echo of the suicide of Müller's wife, Inge, who put her head in the oven at their family home. In the final scene, the line 'Under the sun of torture' is again a direct import, here taken from a short piece Müller wrote on Artaud. Elsewhere, he treats his own work like that of Shakespeare: he skews the transfer. When the Hamlet figure says 'LIKE A HUMP I'M LUGGING MY HEAVY BRAIN' (87), he draws on the formulation 'my head is my hump[back]', spoken by the Hamlet-like character Hasselbein, in *The Building Site* (1965). Here it is not so much the difference between the two formulations that is of interest – they are similar enough to each other – rather that Müller is placing himself and acknowledging his place in his own recycling of the Shakespearean tradition. However, this suggestion may not be quite as hubristic as it sounds. He is perhaps noting that the problems he seeks to confront in *The Hamletmachine* are ones that have concerned him for much longer.

Müller's textual practices do not follow patterns or offer simple ways to unlock them. At times he quotes directly, at others he retains only a hint of an original source. The relationship between a source and its manifestation in the play often creates space for interpretation and speculation. Müller champions the potential of his material to spark associations. This is one basis for the openness of the text, and I will return to the implications of this strategy in the next chapter.

A dense, suggestive texture

The Hamletmachine is replete with a sense of its own insinuation in contexts that pre-exist it. The volley of fragments that form the second section of 'Family Album' confront the audience with such diverse material that the audience cannot but accept that it is dealing with a profoundly unstable text that is drawing on a number of sources. Yet even before this assemblage of fragments, the opening section peppers the audience with strange voices, capitalized for the reader. The tone is set in the second line of the play: 'I stood at the waterfront and talked to the surf BLAH BLAH BLAH, behind me the ruins of Europe' (87). The first part of the line is possibly an allusion to the ancient Greek orator Demosthenes, who, according to Plutarch at least, addressed the waves with a mouthful of pebbles to hone his vocal projection. The subsequent dismissal of what was being said may remind us of Hamlet's reply to Polonius's question, 'What do you read, my lord?': 'Words, words, words' (II.ii.188–9). The final part of the line is an example of the rhetorical trope known as a *mise-en-abîme*. This is when a work signals in one place what it is doing elsewhere. Thus, *The Hamletmachine* could be understood as 'the ruins of Europe', a collection of references, quotations and allusions taken from the continent's cultural, social and historical past. As seen above, the references themselves are often ruined or disfigured; do they become mere 'BLAH BLAH BLAH' or something more meaningful? The question is not quite as facile as it may seem: the response to Müller's play could easily be one of rejection in the face of a plethora of fragments. Taken together, the three parts of the single sentence do a great deal of work. And the sentence itself is not unrepresentative of several others in the play.

This richness runs the risk of overwhelming the
ence. But it also opens up the texts for closer scrutiny
encourages the audience to engage with the associations th
play either deliberately or inadvertently brings forth. As such,
the text can be understood as activating spectators. Take, for
example, the line in 'Family Album' in which the Hamlet figure addresses the Ghost: 'I know you've got one hole too
many. I wish my mother had had one less when you were still
dressed in flesh; it would have spared me myself' (87). One
may detect a similarity to Hamlet's lines: 'The time is out of
joint; O cursed spite / That ever I was born to set it right!'
(I.v.186–7). Alternatively, it may send one to another passage,
later in the play, when Hamlet says: 'I am myself indiffer-
ent honest but yet I could accuse me of such things that it
were better my mother had not borne me' (III.i.121–3). Yet
there are other echoes present, too. The philosopher Friedrich
Nietzsche's first major work, *The Birth of Tragedy*, recounts the
Greek legend of when King Midas seeks out the companion
of Dionysus, Silenus. On finally apprehending him, the King
asks what the best thing for a human being might be. Silenus
replies that the answer is impossible, as the best thing is never
to have been born. Thus, in one allusion, one may find shades
of *Hamlet*, a reference to an ancient myth and its reuse in
one of the most well-known books of a significant philosopher. However, there is no direct textual reference to *Hamlet*,
Silenus or Nietzsche, and so, in a play as densely stocked with
material as this, associations can be multiply resonant.

Comprende?

I could list several more examples that draw on even more
Shakespeare and reference T. S. Eliot, Joseph Conrad, Walter

...burg, Boris Pasternak, the Lord's Prayer
...others. Such is the wealth of material
...each from the ancient Greeks, via the
...ers and more recent history sets out
...short piece of writing.

...wever, other instances in which the sources
...proven elusive to identify. Some lines in 'Family Album'
are signalled as 'foreign' because they are presented in block
capitals, although scholars have never been able to link them
to either a direct or indirect source. 'YOU'RE TOO LATE
MY FRIEND TO COLLECT YOUR FEE / NO PLACE
FOR YOU IN MY TRAGEDY' (88) sounds like a line
from another play or perhaps a song; 'MOTHER'S WOMB
IS NOT A ONE-WAY STREET' (88) is sententious, but
has a more modern ring to it with its inclusion of terminol-
ogy taken from road traffic. In 1995, Müller reflected: 'I've
enjoyed making use of quotations, but I've also enjoyed
making them up.'[2] Here he was referring to the line 'HOW
TO GET RID OF THIS MOST WICKED BODY', which
appears towards the end of his play *Quartet*.[3] The format, the
same as that of the examples taken from *The Hamletmachine*,
deliberately signals textual otherness and suggests the import-
ing practices found elsewhere in the play. So, is Müller merely
playing a game with us and showing how clever he is? While
this is a potential reading, it would seem unlikely. The references and allusions Müller makes throughout the text mix
outright familiarity (e.g. *Richard III*), something recognizable
(much of the manipulation of *Hamlet*) and material that is
more obscure (who knows about Demosthenes nowadays?).
The addition of invented lines that do not neatly fit into the
text can be understood as further complicating the texture
of the writing. Such a move on Müller's part says something

important about both his use of outside sources and our role as readers and spectators.

A central element of Müller's writing practice is that he is not presenting us with an even, settled text. It consciously signals its debt to a wealth of influences and historical moments, and does not pretend to be the product of an individual. In the first instance, then, the aim is to show that contemporary writing and the contemporary moment are not in some way 'original', but are the result of a series of historical processes. This does not, however, imply that the present is simply a mechanical product of the past: rather, that the past plays an important role in the way we behave in the present, but that that role may not be unambiguous. For example, a central problem in the play is that the Hamlet figure assumes the role of the father he detests: making the same mistake twice is something that history should teach us to avoid. However, the multiplicity of elements from the past make simple causal links between influence and outcome problematic. *The Hamletmachine* can thus be read as a complex meditation on action and the factors that inform it. The 'invented' quotations are another manifestation of the network of sometimes unconscious elements that inform the present.

Yet they play another role, too, and in order to understand this, it is worth considering the idea of allegory. An allegory reprocesses one set of ideas, people and/or events in the form of another. John Bunyan's *The Pilgrim's Progress* mirrors the story of Christian salvation from the 'City of Destruction' (the sinful material world) to the 'Celestial City' (heaven); George Orwell's *Animal Farm* reflects on the history of the Russian Revolution. A problem with allegory is that it can become a kind of guessing game, a hunt to identify the correct correlation between art and life. The work involved in connecting the two can detract from the value of the work itself. By extension, *The Hamletmachine* could become little more than a hunt to identify or uncover the rich network of references and allusions made in the play. At one level, the inclusion of invented sources undermines this endeavour; at another, it makes it null and void.

Instead, Müller may be more interested in the effects the various fragments have upon the reader or spectator. The pointlessness of the 'source hunt' is replaced by a more productive engagement with a profoundly uneven text. It is relatively unimportant whether one knows the provenance of an obscure reference; the more pressing issue is the confrontation with material that does not fit neatly into the texture of the play. In the same interview of 1975, mentioned above, Müller stated: 'when I'm writing, I always have the need to throw as much at people as possible so that they don't know what they should deal with first, and I think that's the only way. . . . I think you can only overwhelm them.'[4] The hope here is not to set the audience an intellectual puzzle, but to encourage them to make choices about what they engage with. This is a more subliminal strategy, one concerned with making the audience active in the face of multiple impulses. Spectators find themselves in moments of crisis where they are not being told how to think or what conclusions to draw. Instead they are faced with an avalanche of diverse material and are invited to develop a relationship with it. There is potentially too much to take in, and so they have to be actively selective.

Consequently, Müller's is not some kind of purely intellectual theatre: the rational mind is being circumvented because it cannot deal with the wealth of material on offer. This has a thematic correlation with *The Hamletmachine* as well. The Hamlet figure is an intellectual, weighing up potentially right and wrong courses of action, drawing on his learning and, ultimately, reverting to the mistakes of his father. This is not unlike Shakespeare's Hamlet, who ends up responding to one murder with a bloodbath of his own. Fortinbras may well praise the dead prince for what he could have done in the future in the final speech of the play ('Bear Hamlet like a soldier to the stage, / For he was likely, had he been put on, / To have proved most royal' (V.ii.380–2)), but what he did hardly dealt with the problems of the present. The rational mind does not exist as a disembodied consciousness and does not make decisions in a vacuum. Müller acknowledges this in his play and tries to force the audience to experience a rush of sensations that overwhelm the rational mind. It is not, however, that he is calling for a reborn Theatre of the Absurd, in which the meaningfulness of existence is underplayed or rejected. The material Müller is discussing is obviously significant: he is dealing with the possibility of action in history, yet he understands that making decisions is often not purely a cerebral matter. The themes of the play are thus built into the fabric of the play's dramaturgy. The audience cannot make rational choices when the material that pervades the text is so difficult to comprehend and assimilate.

Everybody does it

What may emerge from the descriptions of the scenes in Chapter 1 is that there are clear contrasts between the ones with the Hamlet figure (1 and 4) and those that feature Ophelia (2 and 5). The first pair are lengthy, have noticeably uneven textures and are difficult to navigate (for either an actor or a spectator). The second pair are short and more coherent. As already noted, however, the apparent opposition is already undone by Müller's naming practices: the first scene carries no attribution of character to text and the fourth represents a series of denials of who is actually speaking. The second scene has a surfeit of attribution and the fifth opens with a transformation. However, an inspection of the scenes' textual practices also reveals that simple divisions between a Hamlet and an Ophelia are not possible.

It is clear from Scenes 1 and 4 that the Hamlet figure is fundamentally riven. The fragmentary shards of text undermine any sense of unity and stability. The Hamlet figure soaks up material from the past and passes it on to the audience unadorned and jagged. Ophelia, on the other hand, appears to offer greater stability, primarily through the more coherent, seemingly programmatic nature of her two speeches. Yet a closer examination reveals that this superficial coherence is built upon its own accumulation of fragments.

I have already noted that 'Europe of the Woman' opens with a list of female suicides taken from Müller's own writing. The actions that follow – the destruction of the domestic sphere – are also reminiscent of a prominent figure in the West Germany of the early 1970s. The Red Army Faction, also known more popularly as the Baader-Meinhof Gang, was a group of left-wing urban terrorists. Ulrike Meinhof had behaved in ways similar to the Ophelia figure, and so the actions described in the scene also lose their aura of authenticity: she is repeating and varying the deeds of one of the most infamous women in recent German history.[5]

The final scene opens with a literary reference to Greek mythology and drama in the figure of Electra. It is followed by the title of arguably Joseph Conrad's best-known novel, *Heart of Darkness*, and, as mentioned above, a line from a text by Müller on Artaud. The slogan 'Long live hatred, contempt, uprising, death' (94) is not dissimilar to those of the right-wing Falangists of the Spanish Civil War (and today perhaps suggests the sentiments of Islamist terrorists). These associations are important: Müller, as will be discussed in the following chapter, was a Marxist of sorts, someone on the left wing of politics. Yet he connects the more positive figure of Ophelia with nihilistic slogans of the right. He is thus not writing some form of propaganda by holding Ophelia up as an idealized response to the Hamlet complex. She is also sullied and her course of action cannot be accepted without caveat. The final sentence is a direct quotation from Susan Atkins, a member of the 'Family' inspired by Charles Manson to commit a series of unprovoked murders in 1969. Müller apparently read the line by chance in *Life* magazine. It does not appear in block capitals, but does have a jarring effect in the text, potentially signalling its 'foreign' origin.

In short, the Ophelia figure is composed in a similar way to the Hamlet figure: they are both constructions, taken from the clash of a contemporary sensibility and a host of diverse materials. Ophelia's consistency and coherence are superficial, and she, too, is the product of a number of contradictory impulses. The Ophelia figure cannot be simplistically contrasted with the Hamlet figure, and this has an effect on her presentation in performance. Both figures are amalgams, and this status can be revealed on stage: the text does not segregate the two complexes, and a production that suggests such a division has misunderstood Müller's textual strategies.

The Hamletmachine explores issues of human agency and the way that decisions are made at critical points of one's life. The Hamlet figure is charged with avenging his father and is also confronted with responding to political change and revolution. Ophelia chooses to reject the society that has led to her own suicide. One of the many consequences of Müller's textual dramaturgy is that choices are never made in a vacuum. The fragments of text that inhabit the speeches attack the autonomy of the speakers. They utter lines from other people, are pervaded by events from other times and places, and struggle to assert themselves. The play is a meditation in miniature on the difficulty of achieving political ends. Its economy of words and its density of source material make for a pared-down assault on a simple reception of the figures' views and perspectives. In a handful of pages, Müller addresses political realities with which we are all familiar: the cleavage between means and ends, idealism and pragmatism, intention and effect. His extensive use of source material qualifies the figures' existence in the here-and-now, and reintegrates history in its broadest sense into the kaleidoscope of their being. In doing so, Müller suggests that the problems of the past cannot be denied or repressed if they are to be overcome in the present.

Notes

1 This and all subsequent references are taken from William Shakespeare, *Hamlet*, The Arden Shakespeare, Third Series, eds Ann Thompson and Neil Taylor (London: Bloomsbury, 2006).
2 Heiner Müller, in David Barnett, '"Ich erfinde gerne Zitate": Ein Interview mit Heiner Müller', *GDR Bulletin* 22:2 (1995), 9–13 (p. 13).
3 Heiner Müller, *Quartet*, in *Theatremachine*, pp. 103–21 (p. 120). The quotation appears in English in the German original.
4 Heiner Müller, in Laube, 'Literatur', p. 60.
5 References to both the Red Army Faction and Meinhof herself can be found in Müller's notes to the play, located in his archive, e.g. items 3895 or 3888.

3

Open sesame?

It is difficult to overlook just how radical a text *The Hamletmachine* is. Its deliberate problematization of who is speaking, the erosion of plotting, the unorthodox use of language, and references to a slew of wide and varied sources all contribute to a most unusual dramaturgy. This poses a number of questions to anyone seeking to engage with the play, either as reader, maker or spectator. This chapter explores the options available to theatre-makers by considering the nature of drama and the 'open' text, and then proceeds to examine the politics of such openness.

A dramatic pause

As a play, *The Hamletmachine* presents a set of problems for anyone dealing with it because it does not conform to the representational forms associated with drama. Indeed, the term 'drama' itself is difficult to apply to the text and requires definition if we are to understand how Müller diverges from it. Hans-Thies Lehmann's major study, *Postdramatic Theatre*, helps demarcate a play from a drama, and he notes: 'drama means a flow of time, controlled and surveyable'.[1] This brief definition hides a number of ideas that are worth discussing further.

Structuring time imposes order upon chaos. Drama is selective in its treatment of reality and extracts the most salient points and moments for representation. Every line of dialogue has a function in ways that every line of speech may not in our everyday lives. The control of dramatic material is thus a way of creating a logical unfolding of events. On the contrary, events *we* encounter often lack beginnings, middles and ends, yet drama tends to introduce conflicts, develop them and reach denouements. In short, structured time leads to the development of plot and sub-plot, as well as tension and its relief.

Lehmann also considers the 'surveyability' of a drama important. If something is surveyable it is mappable, its dimensions can be measured: the twists and turns of a plot ultimately lead to understanding, and understanding implies a relationship between the play and the world. This 'understanding' is brought about by the process of representation.

Representation is central to drama: one thing stands in for another. An actor represents a character, a set a location, props objects, and the list continues on through all theatre's signifying media. Representation comes in many different forms. Late nineteenth-century realism tried to imitate the world we encounter every day and developed training for actors that sought to bring authenticity and not staginess to the theatre. The drama of the Renaissance was also engaged in representation, but employed other means: no-one speaks like Hamlet, either in his sustained use of poetic language or in metre. All the same, he represents the problems of the drama, together with the rest of the cast.

What can be made, then, of *The Hamletmachine* when viewed as a drama? In terms of representation, it is difficult to know what or who is being represented. Are we even looking at individuals in this play? The history of drama is certainly peppered with authors who have preferred to write 'types' rather than individuated 'characters': restoration comedy embraced social types, the *commedia dell'arte* relied on stock characters, and the Expressionists preferred generic terms like 'the Lady' or 'the Young Man' even in major roles. Yet all these generalized figures still offered forms of personified definition that permitted interpersonal communication and the propulsion of plot.

Müller is, however, articulating something that cannot be pinned down to even a generalized individual. I have chosen to refer to the speakers of the speeches as 'figures' or 'complexes' in previous chapters rather than 'characters' or 'types'. A 'character' is tied to a set of individual qualities that, however contradictory they may be, can still be located in a single person. A 'type' may move beyond the individual to combine a series of traits in a single person, but Müller undermines this conception, too. In the first instance, he refuses to attach a name to the speaker of the first scene. This decision already disconnects the words from a discrete person and invites us to think beyond the confines of the individual. The multiple speakers of the second scene hardly clarify matters, and so it can be said that the play engages with two complexes of ideas, opinions and attitudes. As noted in the previous chapter, the two are neither distinct nor clear-cut, because of their common composite construction. The inscrutable nature of the speakers thus resists the strategies of representation common to the broad practices of drama.

Time is organized in *The Hamletmachine*, but only loosely. There is a certain sequential order in the play: 'Family Album' introduces the Hamlet role before it is rejected in

'Pest in Buda'. 'Europe of the Woman' precedes 'Maddening Endurance', in a movement from the rejection of the present to a call for action. The 'Scherzo' is an episode that sits in the middle of *The Hamletmachine*, in-between scenes dedicated to Hamlet and Ophelia, yet it could hardly be said to have an effect on the flow of the action. Indeed, action as a category is distinctly lacking in the play as a whole. Scenes 3, 4 and 5 all contain 'action' in that the stage directions seem to be telling us that states are changing, yet, as noted in Chapter 1, the directions themselves are more metaphorical than literal. So, it is perhaps the case that nothing 'happens' as such.

Nonetheless, drama has endured despite the lack of causal connection between different scenes. Episodic drama tends to do one of two things: it progresses through time, picking out the most significant events of a character's life or characters' lives; or it offers a series of scenes that are unrelated by action, but associatively related by theme. So, can *The Hamletmachine* be understood as a series of episodes? While they are certainly linked thematically, the scenes themselves do not really 'progress'. Rather, they offer a detailed description of a set of states that are pervaded by material from the past. A state may be replete with contradictory impulses, yet it is essentially static. It is thus difficult to conclude that the scenes are episodes at all.

It would seem that *The Hamletmachine* cannot be considered a drama under the criteria that apply to even more experimental pieces. Its relationship to representation is questionable and it does not structure time in the way drama usually does to create tension and pressure. This change in status is important, as it has an effect on the way that theatre-makers may approach the play.

Degrees of openness

All texts written for theatrical performance are open, if 'open' means that they allow a creative interaction when moving from page to stage. We will never see the same *Hamlet* in different stagings, and our imagining of a potential production will always differ from the real thing on stage. The reason for this is obvious: a text and a production are two categorically distinct entities, and the former is unable to encode sufficiently precise instructions for a seamless transformation to the latter, however detailed its stage directions may be. This is hardly a controversial argument, yet there is clearly a relationship between a text and its performance that has provoked much discussion about whether a production has adequately staged its text. Playwrights have often complained about how directors 'hijack' their texts in the pursuit of a personal vision of a work. Elsewhere critics may bemoan discrepancies between how a character or a scene has been written and how it appears on stage. Such differences of opinion are sometimes located in the text and are sometimes a matter of taste, and it is not the place here to arbitrate on particular disagreements. At present it suffices to say that openness in a dramatic text is largely a question of interpretation, of how one chooses to represent the text in practice.

What, then, can be made of 'openness' when representation itself is called into question? On the one hand, *The Hamletmachine* is a profoundly open text because it offers so little restriction to theatre-makers' imaginations. The speeches do not map onto individuals or types, action defers to states, and even the stage directions may not be intended to be realized literally. In short, the play appears to offer production teams a great deal of latitude. Yet, on closer inspection, it may also be making a set of demands.

If *The Hamletmachine* is not concerned with representing characters and actions, then a production that seeks to interpret the material on stage is 'closing' the openness of the text. The play thus invites theatre-makers to respect its openness, not by reducing it, but by retaining it. This, ironically, is itself a restriction. The play asks its realizers to challenge their conventional practices and develop new ones. This was Müller's thrust when arguing that it was literature's task to resist the institution of the theatre, noted in Chapter 1.

Retaining the openness of the text is not something that is without its own parameters. Every time a play is staged, be it the most derivative mega-musical or most challenging experimental piece, it is in dialogue with its times and its society. This may mean staging a production that sells lots of tickets, yet even that kind of venture needs to be sensitive to the spectating habits of its audience: a hit in one place may prove a flop in another. Other kinds of theatre, such as the revival of a classic text, might seek a contemporary resonance or prefer to offer a rigorous treatment of the material itself to contrast original practices with the expectations of contemporary theatre. In each case, success is the product of a careful negotiation among a number of variables, and the same is true of plays like *The Hamletmachine*. It may be a radically open text, yet openness itself comes in many forms.

A politics in the chaos

Written in 1977, *The Hamletmachine* has been aligned with what is broadly called postmodernism. Definitions of this term are many and various, and it would be a forlorn task to articulate them all here: a brief summary will have to suffice.

Modernism in the arts is often associated with a set of intellectual earthquakes that undermined previously held certainties. Albert Einstein's relativity questioned whether we can know the value of absolute quantities such as the measurement of time, the speed of movement or the length of objects. Sigmund Freud's psychology overthrew the rational basis of decision-making and emphasized uncontrolled human desires. Ferdinand de Saussure's linguistics divorced words from their meaning and posited an arbitrary relationship between the two. Karl Marx's sociology criticized the permanence of social structures and human nature. Friedrich Nietzsche's philosophy attacked a sense of stability in morality and proposed that our values were always in a state of transformation. The effects of these ideas and discoveries, among others, provoked a crisis of representation in the arts, or modernism as it has become known. Modernism was the shock of the new, a response to upheavals in what can be known about the world in an absolute way. The outcomes were many and varied, with some artists embracing the new possibilities and others clinging to old certainties. What was shocking and new to the modernists has become the norm to postmodernists.

In the light of this rather condensed definition, *The Hamletmachine* can be understood as a postmodern play, alive with the chaos of the postmodern condition. It is constructed of fragments whose final meaning is unknowable, and it presents them in forms that do not point to any definitive meaning. The sheer number of competing impulses refuses to guarantee sound interpretation, and the figures themselves are models of decentredness. As such, the play can be understood as a kind of naturalism, a photograph of contemporary reality that does not seek to make the meaningful connections associated with drama.

The problem of action in the play also suggests that history seems to have stopped, a postmodern claim that proposes that we live in a perpetual present in which nothing really changes. This position appears to be underlined by the final lines of the fourth scene, in which the slaughter of Marx, Lenin and Mao induces an ice age, and the stasis of the final scene, in which the voice of opposition is brought to silence. As a result, the play can be considered a deeply pessimistic one, in which all hope is extinguished and the figures are condemned to remain trapped in their time, frozen for eternity. Postmodernity is never to be overcome.

Yet *The Hamletmachine* can be read in an altogether different way, one that is more dynamic and progressive. In order to understand this position, it is necessary to examine Müller's relationship to one of the most significant figures in twentieth-century theatre, Bertolt Brecht.

Brecht's greatest contribution to theatre was perhaps his theories and practices of staging reality dialectically. Dialectics, an idea developed principally by the philosopher Hegel, proposes that reality is not stable, but is defined by the clash of entities whose relationship is defined by contradiction. When a contradiction becomes too great, change ensues. Marx interpreted movements in societies through history dialectically, and his ideas paved the way for revolutionary practice. That is, by viewing the world as defined by contradiction rather than coherence, he understood the world as fundamentally changeable: one has to identify contradictions and make use of them as a motor for change. Brecht, following Marx, sought ways to imbue dramatic representation with the impetus of dialectics.

Dialectical theatre focuses on articulating and perf(contradiction. As Brecht once put it: 'Contradictions are our hope!'.[2] This optimistic slogan rests on the belief that no situation can remain the same; it will change because contradictions cannot persist in perpetuity. History bears this out: one need only look at attitudes towards slavery, child labour or the disenfranchisement of women to see how attitudes and, more importantly, behaviour have changed over time. Yet, change is not always a good thing. It can be argued that the all-engulfing encroachment of globalization and the pervasiveness of capitalism after the collapse of communism in the early 1990s led to the global economic crisis of 2007–8. To a dialectician, it is the phenomenon of change that has remained constant, and this suggests that we are not living in a perpetual present, as postmodernism would have it, but one that is still capable of transformation. After all, it would be fanciful to contend that the world is somehow free of contradiction.

Dialectics is concerned with relationships (based on contradiction) and processes (overcoming contradiction and engendering change). As a result, 'things' do not exist in isolation and are revealed to be interdependent and interrelated. That is, everything is in dialogue with its social and historical context and will often prove to be a contradictory entity itself because it has changed so much over its lifetime. Take, for instance, the example of globalization as a contradictory whole. On the one hand, it has broken down borders and boundaries, making communication easier and faster; on the other, a crisis in one place can spread to others with greater speed, causing greater damage. This phenomenon is thus both positive and negative, and any attempt to resolve its contradictions has to be holistic. A current problem, the spread of Islamist terrorism, cannot simply be dealt with by attacking its symptoms, according to dialecticians. The bid to eradicate or weaken Al-Qaida, for example, may have been successful, but the so-called Islamic State has entered the vacuum and taken its place. The causes of such terrorism are more complex than their manifestations in named organizations, and unless the causes are confronted together, the diminution of one group will not see the end of the forces that brought about its creation in the first place.

Brecht's dialectical theatre was thus concerned not only with staging contradiction, but with dramatizing processes. The title figure in *Mother Courage and Her Children* is portrayed in a variety of ways: in one scene she curses the war that has robbed her of a son, in the next she celebrates it because her business is doing well. Are we to praise or condemn her? This is the wrong question: her behaviour is always linked to her situation. We thus have to consider how to change the situation so that it might have a more beneficent effect on her actions and opinions.

How, then, might a play as radical as *The Hamletmachine* be understood as dialectical theatre? Müller, in an oft-quoted line that ended a talk delivered at the International Brecht Society in 1979, asserted: 'To use Brecht without criticizing him is betrayal.'[3] The ideas that informed this conclusion were that Brecht's later work, for which he is known around the world, is too restricted; it does not engage with reality as reality appears to us, but imposes forms and ideas upon it; it is too restricted. Müller's counterexample is Franz Kafka, whose work 'describes gestures without a reference system'.[4] That is, Kafka does not offer a key to understanding his literature; it is the reader's job to negotiate its meaning and its problems. Müller also notes how the Left's (and by extension Brecht's) emphasis on rationalism has exposed it to the ravages of a

conservatism that is happy to champio⸍
achieve its ends, as was the case with the
of these positions, it can be said that Mu⸌⸌
Brecht, but proposes that his ideas and his practic⸌⸌
be rethought.

If Brecht still survives in *The Hamletmachine*, then where is
he to be found? The focus on contradiction, the motor of the
dialectic, is still visible. The many fragments that inform the
text are set out, but never harmonized. The Hamlet figure is
constituted by contradictory impulses, yet these are not in
some way arbitrary. The references to nuggets of history –
the Hungarian Uprising of 1956, consumerism, the Berlin
Wall – anchor the problems in concrete contexts. A relationship is established between a shifting set of material conditions and the manifestations of reality that run through the
play. The Hamlet figure would not be struggling with a series
of political challenges without the figures of Marx, Lenin
and Mao that he beheads at the end of the fourth scene,
for example. The renaissance protagonist is not a model of
timeless indecision: he is placed firmly in the present of the
play, confronting political questions of action, change and
revolution.

The end of the play, which seems so hopeless in its postmodern reading, becomes something else when read dialectically. Yes, the final images are ones of stasis, but this state is one
that is the product of the contradictions that run through every
scene. In this context, it is worth noting Müller's comment,
made eight years after writing *The Hamletmachine*: 'shame-
less, the lie of POSTHISTOIRE before the barbaric reality of our prehistory'.[5] That is, Müller notes that history
has not reached an end point, although he acknowledges
that the problems of the play will persist without new ideas

and actions. Like globalization or terrorism, they have to be approached as a contradictory, dialectical whole. The final image is thus not a resigned sigh, but a provocation. Brecht's optimism ('Contradictions are our hope!') underpins the bleak finale – the fact that the world cannot remain as it is is ultimately a productive impulse nestled into workings of *The Hamletmachine*.

Brecht's dialectic, as instanced in the example of Mother Courage, above, implicitly suggests that a move from capitalism to socialism will help alleviate the dilemmas the character faces. While Müller was a Marxist, he was sceptical about the conclusions Brecht had drawn. He noted approvingly: 'Marx didn't devise a system; on the contrary, he worked on negation, on a critique of the existing state of affairs. Consequently, he was open to new realities in principle.'[6] Müller's dialectical logic is thus not so much focused on the realization of a utopia in the first instance, but on stockpiling contradictions without knowing what will take their place. In this sense, he is a dialectical diagnostician, assessing a rotten state of affairs. The contradictions he articulates are, however, presented in such a way that it is not the stage that points to solutions; that is the work of the spectators.

This refusal to point to solutions on the part of the playwright does not, however, betoken some kind of resignation. Instead, it is a mark of humility: he does not have the answers or know a better way. Yet his dramaturgical form, that of serving up dialectical contradictions, suggests that the states depicted in the play cannot endure, however much they may threaten to. The sense that this situation is to continue *ad infinitum* is resisted by the contradictions that brought it about. Müller thus replaces postmodern chaos with a more nuanced post-Brechtian dramaturgy. His refusal to limit the Hamlet and Ophelia complexes to individuals opens up the contradictory impulses that pervade them. The careful integration of historical material puts them into a variety of frames of reference, but again, these do not limit interpretation; rather they contextualize the conflicts that run through the play.

Müller performs a dialectical twist by presenting a play that appears to be one pervaded by pessimism and revealing it as one that is predicated on change. The postdramatic 'states' that describe each scene are dynamic products of dialectical tensions. For example, the Hamlet figure, rejecting Shakespeare's *Hamlet*, does not pay tribute to his murdered father, but condemns him as a murderous vestige of another age. Yet by the end of the play, he has assumed his father's mantle. A process has taken place and reached an end point, and the audience is invited to ask why this happened and how it might be avoided. The text is too alive with contradiction to be read as a meditation on an inevitable conservatism on Hamlet's part that will always lead to paralysis. The Ophelia figure is a challenge to this reading, but she, too, has to be confronted: for all her revolutionary energy, she is not an undilutedly positive figure. The post-Brechtian desire to present the world dialectically, but to leave the dialectics open, runs through *The Hamletmachine*, and it is the theatre's task to rise to such a challenge.

Notes

1 Hans-Thies Lehmann, *Postdramatic Theatre*, trans. Karen Jürs-Munby (Abingdon: Routledge, 2006), p. 40.
2 Bertolt Brecht, *The Threepenny Lawsuit*, in *Brecht on Film and Radio*, ed. Marc Silberman (London: Methuen, 2001), p. 148.

3 Heiner Müller, 'Brecht vs. Brecht', in *Germania*, ed. Lotringer, pp. 124–32 (p. 133).

4 Ibid., p. 125.

5 Heiner Müller, 'Die Wunde Woyzeck', in Müller, *Werke*, Vol. VIII, ed. Frank Hörnigk (Frankfurt am Main: Suhrkamp, 2005), pp. 281–3 (p. 282).

6 Heiner Müller, 'Da trinke ich lieber Benzin zum Frühstück', in Müller, *Werke*, Vol. XI, ed. Frank Hörnigk (Frankfurt am Main: Suhrkamp, 2008), pp. 431–45 (p. 432).

Staging *The Hamletmachine*

The production history of *The Hamletmachine* is a little odd in that it began with a couple of failed attempts before theatre-makers realized the possibilities that resided in the complex play; numerous innovative stagings followed. One of these failed attempts reveals the problems of remaining trapped in the ways of theatrical convention. The abandoned rehearsals for the world premiere of the play in Cologne in 1978 reveal that a major contributory factor for the cancellation can be found in the rationalist stance of the actor playing the Hamlet figure. He considered the play 'a normal, an understandable, explicable, interpretable play'.[1] The belief that such scenes can simply be unpacked and approached with the actor's conventional tools led to intractable impasses. The text openly resists attempts to limit its meaning by interpreting its lines, as even a cursory reading of the speeches reveals.

In this chapter, I will be describing and analysing two very different productions of the play. They reveal the range of possibilities available to theatre-makers who accept that this type of open text need not be interpreted on stage, but can nonetheless have meaning by imaginatively deferring that activity to the spectators. I have chosen the two productions from many, many examples because they demonstrate two distinct points of entry: the first could be considered a detached treatment of the text, the second a more personal engagement.

A machine aesthetic

Robert Wilson is an internationally fêted director of theatre and opera. His work is well known for a number of qualities: his scenes emphasize the passing of time; he treats different sign-systems (e.g. text, movement, lighting) as autonomous entities; and his performers tend to be subjugated to the director's instructions, rather than using the stage as a site for self-expression. While I could discuss any of these features in greater detail, I shall instead consider their deployment in Wilson's production of *The Hamletmachine* that premiered in May 1986 with a group of students from New York University.

Rehearsals began not with the text, but with a series of movements. The movements involved all fifteen performers and cannot be described here because the sequence and its gestures are too complicated, involved too many people and lasted for about twenty minutes. Wilson moved the sequence on using resonant wooden sticks as a cue for the next movement. In the finished piece, the sequence was performed five times in total and the production lasted for almost two and a half hours. What is worth noting is that the sequence was rehearsed to a satisfactory level before the first word of the play was ever spoken.

The stage was bounded by three curtains and a back wall; the four sides formed a trapezium. The curtains opened and the first twenty or so minutes presented only the sequence of movements and gestures. Each change was signalled by the click of the wooden sticks. Once the sequence was over, the curtains were drawn and all the performers moved clockwise through ninety degrees. The curtains were reopened, and the performers moved through the same sequence, yet this time, the text of 'Family Album' was spoken by different voices. As a result, some parts of the sequence were stretched while others were truncated to allow the full text to be delivered by the various performers. The same ninety-degree rotation and careful integration of the respective texts recurred in 'Europe of the Woman', 'Pest in Buda' and 'Maddening Endurance', so that by the final scene, the performers had come full circle and were in the same positions as for the opening dumb show. The audience was thus introduced to the sequence and observed its four subsequent repetitions. Each iteration altered the way the sequence was treated so that it attained the status of a language. Spectators could thus start to detect the play of similarity and difference, and ask why certain variations occurred at certain times.

The treatment of the texts already signals language's special status in the production: it was not the focus and it did not define what happened on stage. Rather, it exercised a pressure on the sequence, extending certain moments and compressing others. Text in dramatic theatre tends to determine the shape of a production; inflection, movement, set, costume and lighting are often subordinated to spoken language in order to support its articulation. In Wilson's production, language was dethroned and integrated into the show as a whole. This change in status reflects the point noted in Chapter 1, that language may be 'speaking' us and not vice versa. In other words, human agency was radically questioned as the performers began to resemble automata and not individuals.

The texts were not spoken in a monotone, however, although it would be difficult to assert that each line had its own 'character'. A dry neutrality tended to dominate 'Family Album', for example, but the capitalized lines elicited more mannered deliveries, and some lines were repeatedly screeched at the audience. In the imagined rape of Gertrude, the lines were delivered word by word by different performers, something that increased the tension without any commensurate emphasis in their voices. In 'Europe of the Woman', by contrast, one performer spoke most of the lines, while another punctuated the scene with the repeated line 'SNOW ON HER LIPS' (89). Three women sitting at a table said their lines in different voices. Male weeping and sobbing accompanied the latter part of the speech.

These two examples show the ways in which the Hamlet and Ophelia complexes were treated differently, yet a common approach underlay them: there was no attempt to connect the text to an individual. The scene's lines worked their way through the movement sequences and produced different responses. 'Family Album' was more linear; the lines were passed from one male voice to the next. 'Europe of the Woman' presented a rich, fugue-like quality, with the different voices speaking singularly and then as a chorus of sorts. The addition of the male laments corresponded to the direction 'OPHELIA [CHORUS/HAMLET]' (89), but in a way that arose from Wilson's directorial plan, not the text's.

The 'Scherzo' played up to the grotesque nature of the scene, but diverged from the pattern developed in the rest of the production. For the most part, a projected film was shown on the back wall. The scene featured no spoken words: the text scrolled across the screen from right to left. The only sound was a recording of the opera singer Jessye Norman

singing Schubert's 'The Dwarf'. The performers appeared
pre-filmed on the screen while they remained still on stage.
The men caught fire at the line 'Do you want to eat my
heart, Hamlet' (89) while the women smiled malevolently.
Towards the end of the scene, the women turned into goril-
las, yet by its conclusion the men and women returned to
their opening states. The picture pixelated and shrank, leav-
ing images of blue skies, some clouds and a crashing plane's
fireball. Wilson thus marked the 'Scherzo' as having a special
place in the play, but, again, left it open to interpretation.
There was no attempt to stage the unstageable stage directions, and the changes in the projected images offered no
explanatory help to the audience.

'Pest in Buda' repeated and varied the practices of 'Family
Album', yet it was the female performers who mostly delivered the stage directions. These were thus allowed to unfold
in the audience's imaginations and not on stage. The only
directions that were performed were the ones discussed
above in Chapter 1: '*A photograph of the writer*' and '[the
Hamletperformer] *tears up the photograph of the writer*' (93).
One can only speculate on the meaning of the gesture, but its
performance clearly marks it as something different from the
other stage directions in the play.

Wilson's production very much emphasized the 'machine'
in *The Hamletmachine*. The ninety-degree turns suggested a
movement through time, as each rotation produced a new
variation. There was no sense that any of the performers was
doing anything other than what they were told to do; there
were no 'selves' on stage as such. Yet, as described above, this
was not a production that eschewed emotion or humour.

Wilson has described the two levels of discourse in his
show as a radio play and a silent film, and believed that the

two, while distinct, could have an effect on each other and
reinforce moments of confluence between them.[2] Thus, while
the movement sequence did nothing directly to explicate the
texts, it developed a relationship with them that could bring
out nuance or highlight particular moments.

It may seem odd to couple Müller, a Marxist in the
Brechtian tradition, with the formalist practices of Wilson.
Yet Müller was a great fan of Wilson's work for a number of
reasons. In 1985, after an earlier collaboration, Müller noted:

> What interests me about Wilson . . . is that he gives the
> elements of theatre their freedom. He would never inter-
> pret a text, which is the norm for directors in European
> theatre dealing with texts. . . . It is a democratic under-
> standing of theatre. Interpretation is the spectator's job,
> and that must not take place on stage. The spectator can't
> be robbed of this work. That's consumerism . . . . That's
> capitalist theatre.[3]

Müller links an attitude towards composition to a politics that
goes beyond the subject matter itself. The way that Wilson
frees up the theatrical elements is, to Müller, a democratic
gesture in that the theatre loses its authority to define its own
meanings. Like Müller's texts, Wilson's productions remain
radically open. Yet, also like Müller's texts, it is not that Wilson
has nothing to say; he acknowledges that the material itself
is pointed and challenging, but is not prepared to influence
audience reception directly. Müller calls this 'democratic' in
that it is the audience's 'work' to grapple with the issues and
not to be lectured from the stage. Wilson's directorial practice
does not turn the play into a consumable product, but leaves
it open for further engagement.

A year later, Müller elaborated on his sentiment by contending that 'on [Wilson's] stage . . . Brecht's epic dramaturgy has a space to dance'.[4] The link between dialectical theatre and the work of Robert Wilson is made explicit here and helps us understand Müller's post-Brechtian theatre: while it is still fascinated by contradiction, it does not seek to imply solutions, as Müller believed Brecht's did. Instead, the contradictions can be made to 'dance', to move and make contact with each other beyond the reach of the playwright or the director. Here, the spectator is the only arbiter: the contradictions are presented on stage, but only dealt with in the auditorium, if at all.

The personal is the political

Robert Wilson is a pioneering director with an international reputation, and his *Hamletmachine* ranks as one of his most important productions today. On the contrary, the German director Sabine Andreas is hardly known, unlike such directing greats as Peter Stein, Ruth Berghaus or Frank Castorf, and her production of *The Hamletmachine* has garnered precious little attention over time. Yet it is worth examining her production of the play that opened in the provincial town of Schwerin in October 1993 for the factors that produced a local, but palpable, hit. As will become evident, even though she did not adhere to some of the implications of the text discussed in previous chapters, her work nonetheless demonstrates how a text that has no singular meanings of its own can be affected by the conditions under which it is rehearsed.

Schwerin is a town in what, until 1990, was a part of the German Democratic Republic (GDR). *The Hamletmachine* was written by an East German citizen, yet Andreas was a West

German director.[5] The actors, who were all East German, felt put upon by a representative of the Germany that 'won' the Cold War, and considered the choice of play wrong. Not only did they deem it unstageable, but they also feared that no-one would come and see it. As contracted ensemble members, they participated only to honour their contracts. It was perhaps this tension, of performing the material unwillingly in the first instance, that led to the unexpected success of the production: it ran for seventeen well-attended performances in a provincial town.

The staging took place on a relatively bare stage. A black back wall was punctuated by five black doors, each topped by a triangle, giving each one the feel of a gravestone. While the programme named the figures 'Hamlet', 'Ophelia' and 'Claudius' (who also doubled as 'Horatio'), the texts were not simply delivered as monologues. For 'Family Album', the actor playing Hamlet approached a microphone after a full three minutes of silence on stage. Silence here represented the counterpoint to the difficult texts and also challenged the audience's expectations with respect to the spoken word from the outset. As Hamlet proceeded, Ophelia and the rest of the ensemble would improvise responses to the text, producing different material night by night. As the run progressed, the cast teased out and developed new ideas, and so the production evolved markedly over time.

'Europe of the Woman' acknowledged Müller's directions in that Hamlet entered and started to recite the text as if he were writing it. Only halfway through did Ophelia enter and began delivering the text on her own terms. A chorus of women then joined her, but got stuck on the repeated pronoun 'I'. The treatment of the scene opened up its text as a result of the three different renditions offered. While spectators could probably dismiss Hamlet's version as a botched attempt at sympathy with the women, the tension between Ophelia and the chorus was more difficult to delineate, with the chorus picking up on the individualistic inflection of the speech, something that is in contradiction with the generalizing thrust when Ophelia claims to speak for all European female suicides.

The 'Scherzo', by Andreas's own admission, followed Müller's stage directions too slavishly, and as they became ever diffuse, the production became ever more literal. 'Pest in Buda' was also somewhat literal in that, for example, the three revolutionary classics, Marx, Lenin and Mao, were represented as hallowed Russian church icons (that were then destroyed by Hamlet's axe), yet a more playful approach to delivery was also present. The scene focused on Hamlet's inability to commit to revolutionary politics. In the opening section, the Chinese national anthem played, but Hamlet was unable to raise a clenched fist in support, as the sound of tanks merged with the melody. Later, instead of the photograph of Müller, a visual metaphor appeared on stage: a bottle of whiskey, something closely associated with the author by that time. Instead of destroying it, Hamlet drank it completely. The alcohol thus fired him up as he verbally stumbled through the following speech. 'Maddening Endurance' then offered a rendition that conformed to the written version.

The question is, then, how a production that may not have taken up all of Müller's challenges could be considered a significant counterexample to Wilson's. The answer lies not so much in Andreas's ideas, which were at times inspired and at others a little too conventional, but in the ways in which the actors were allowed to bring their own experiences to their performances. As already noted, there was an unmistakeable tension between director and ensemble, yet she gave the actors the space to express this during their performances. They were encouraged not to interpret lines they felt were too difficult or impenetrable, but to perform their incredulity *and* their discoveries on stage. As a result, reviewers noted something unexpected. One reviewer found 'sporadic fragments of memories from the GDR, associatively interpolated'. Another remarked that *The Hamletmachine* was 'a puzzling piece, yet not so far from reality as we in the West once thought'.[6] The responses show how the interaction between the actors' personal responses and a challenging text can produce engaging theatre, especially for an audience with an open mind and a relationship to the play's material based on their own experiences – in this case as erstwhile East German citizens.

Unforeseen commonalities

It may appear that Wilson's and Andreas's productions represent two ways of approaching *The Hamletmachine* from different ends of the actor's spectrum. Wilson was not interested in the text's meaning as such, and integrated it into an already rehearsed sequence of movements. The actors had virtually no input and were not invited to contribute explicitly. Andreas was involved in something of a tussle to stage the play at all, rubbing up against unwilling actors who worked on the project out of contractual obligation rather than professional enthusiasm. Yet by the time the rehearsals ended, the cast had managed to work the East–West tensions into their performances: the production, in part, became a record of their own encounters with the speeches.

On closer inspection, however, the two productions may have more in common than one might first think. Wilson repeated and varied a series of movements and gestures five times. While the first iteration could give the impression that the actors were carrying out a prescribed sequence, subsequent repetitions actually allowed the audience to note differences between the altered executions of the same movements. Consequently, the actor's input did emerge, and the production was not as 'cold' as its description might suggest. The actors were not exclusively Wilson's playthings: the reprises produced tensions between actor and direction, and allowed the audience to detect the effects of the different texts on similar movements and gestures. As such, Wilson's work inches closer to that of Andreas: both combine the rigour of Müller's open texts with a more personal relationship, and that confrontation can lead to a fascinating play that is present in the play's title: the tension between human being and machine.

Both productions also show the different ways in which meaning itself can be held in abeyance and passed on to the audience. This strategy is clear in Wilson's production: his imposition of text onto movement deliberately held the lines' meaning in check. Andreas also sought to let the words speak for themselves. While the actors' experiences were visible, the texts themselves were not flattened by the operation of character. Andreas preferred to set up different approaches to delivery, especially in the first and second scenes, that destabilized any single reading and opened up a series of choices that the audience was invited to negotiate.

Both productions share two common features: they do not attempt to fathom the meaning of the play *and* they develop the actors' relationship to it. This combination generates a productive point of departure for an audience. On the one hand, spectators are not denied their right, as Müller would see it, to determine their own connections to the play. On the other, they can also respond to the actors' experience of the play, which is different from the actors' interpretation of the play. In neither production were the actors instructed to hide themselves behind the difficult, multilayered lines. This tension suggests a viable treatment of such an open text: it lives from a fascination with the play and its performers.

Notes

1 Gerhard Winter in an interview, in Theo Girshausen (ed.), *'Die Hamletmaschine': Heiner Müllers Endspiel* (Cologne: Prometh, 1978), p. 56.

2 See Robert Wilson, in Knut Hicketier (ed.), *Heiner Müller inszenieren: Unterhaltung im Theater* (Berlin: Die dramaturgische Gesellschaft, 1987), p. 23.

3 Heiner Müller, in Olivier Ortolani, 'Die Form entsteht aus dem Maskieren', in Müller, *Werke*, Vol. X, pp. 346–63 (pp. 361–2).

4 Heiner Müller, 'Taube und Samurai', in Müller, *Werke*, Vol. VIII, ed. Frank Hörnigk (Frankfurt am Main: Suhrkamp, 2005), p. 290.

5 The information for much of the description of the process is taken from an interview I conducted with Andreas on 23 March 1995.

6 Dietrich Pätzold, 'Das Zeitalter verendet als starker Theaterabend', and Horst Köpke, 'Die Macht, die nicht mehr ist', respectively. Both reviews were supplied by Andreas and did not have full bibliographical details.

Conclusion

In the previous chapters I have examined the play's scenes and their challenges, the wealth of sources and their possible functions, the implications of a radically open text and its politics, and two divergent productions and their commonalities. This final section speculates on the future for *The Hamletmachine* as a text for performance.

One of the appeals of the play is its formal complexity and its refusal to offer a clear route from page to stage. Indeed, its images, as encoded in its sometimes visceral language and its stage directions, defy literal interpretation and provoke theatre-makers to experiment with new approaches to staging. In the English-speaking world, the play has proved especially popular in universities, where its form presents a series of novel challenges to students' understandings of what a play can and cannot offer its readers and performers. As such, *The Hamletmachine* represents a never-to-be-fathomed conundrum of a play. However, the question arises as to whether it represents more than just a perplexing exercise for the theatrically curious.

The subject matter and themes are, as in any play, rooted in their time. Much has changed since 1977, when Müller was writing in the midst of the Cold War. The historical backdrop of the clash between socialist and capitalist societies has now passed, and it appears that globalized neoliberal economics has triumphed. Yet what runs through the play is its insistence on contradiction, and this structural feature helps the play move beyond its original context. As history would have it, globalization is having a more difficult time stabilizing itself than had once seemed the case. The world financial crash of 2007–8 has confirmed what many already suspected: that even this version of capitalism is profoundly volatile and can have far-reaching effects that permeate all strata of society. An economic system that promised the wealth and prosperity capitalism has always promised has been exposed by its own mechanisms: the unfettered race to maximize profits for what has become known as 'the one per cent' has huge destructive potential. In this context, *The Hamletmachine* registers its presence.

In general terms, the play resists a trend that has bedded down since the early 1990s. The rise of globalized capitalism has sought to focus minds on a perpetual present and to draw a line under the past. This erasure of historical consciousness is, of course, most useful to a system that presents itself as the only game in town. As Müller put it pithily in a letter to Robert Wilson: 'no revolution without memory'.[1] Without reference points outside any given system, there is no need to challenge, let alone overthrow that system. *The Hamletmachine* is alive with diffuse material, harvested from a wealth of sources that date back to the ancients and the Bible. The emphasis on the role of contradiction and the effort required to neutralize and surmount it speak to the problems of the present quite clearly. The stagnation at the end of the play finds its analogue in the possibility that globalized capitalism may simply go on and on.

More specifically, the play is concerned with the tension between committing to a progressive politics and succumbing to the forces of conservatism. The Hamlet figure, for all his arguments and desires to back revolt, ultimately dons his father's armour and, in doing so, brings about a political ice age. Questions of how change may be brought about and what it might achieve are central to *The Hamletmachine*. Their articulation is always contradictory, as found in both the Hamlet and Ophelia figures, and remains open. On offer is a topography of the problems; only by confronting these in their complexity can spectators formulate strategies for change. The particular instance of socialist revolution (the focus of 'Pest in Buda') now functions more metaphorically in the context of committing to, say, anti-capitalism or environmental activism. Behind all the noble causes are two potential impasses. The Hamlet figure always has his social advantages to fall back on: 'My repulsion / Is a privilege' (92). The Ophelia figure always runs the risk of unleashing uncoordinated violence in a bid to tear down yesterday to build a better tomorrow. Neither route is obviously superior to the other. Hamlet may be easier to condemn than Ophelia, yet in the current climate, she gains the contours of a fundamentalist. (Yet if this is a way she may be understood nowadays, it would be a mistake to dress the Ophelia figure in, say, a burka – a somewhat reductive interpretation for a figure that draws on a considerably broader range of references.)

The Hamletmachine is always suggestive: its form encourages connotation over denotation. Successful productions have fed off this quality and have been content to present rather than to represent the content of the scenes. Productions have manufactured associations grouped around the two imperfect thematic complexes, Hamlet and Ophelia. They open up present-day political dilemmas in such a way that their contradictions are never reconciled, passing on judgement from the cast to the audience. Müller has written a play that, on the surface, appears wilfully obscure and confusing. Its longevity, however, rests on the space created by its form and formulations. It is safe to say that as long as there is a rift between radicalism and conservatism, idealism and pragmatism, there will always be opportunities to read and perform *The Hamletmachine*.

Note

1 Heiner Müller, 'Brief an Robert Wilson', in Müller, *Werke*, Vol. XVIII, pp. 315–18 (p. 315).

Index